About this book

Have you ever wondered why trees don't fall down, how soil is made, or why bees hum? Asking these questions is what being a scientist is all about. This book is about the science that happens around you every day, out in the backyard and in your local park. Keep your eyes open and you'll soon be making your own discoveries.

How?

Why?

What if?

Where?

Hall of Fame

Archie and his friends are here to help you. They are each named after a famous scientist—apart from Bob the (rubber) Duck, who is just a young scientist like you!

Archie

ARCHIMEDES (287–212 B.C.)

The Greek scientist Archimedes figured out why things float or sink while he was in the bathtub. According to the story, he was so pleased that he leaped up, shouting "Eureka!" which means "I've got it!"

Frank

BENJAMIN FRANKLIN (1706–1790)

Besides being one of the most important figures in American history, he was also a noted scientist. In a dangerous experiment in which he flew a kite in a storm, he proved that lightning is actually electricity.

Marie

MARIE CURIE (1867–1934)

Girls did not go to college in Poland where Marie Curie grew up, so she went to Paris to study. Later, she worked on radioactivity and received two Nobel prizes for her discoveries, in 1903 and 1911.

Dot

DOROTHY HODGKIN (1910–1994)

Dorothy Hodgkin was a British scientist, who made many important discoveries about molecules and atoms, the tiny particles that make up everything around us. She was given the Nobel prize for Chemistry in 1964.

At Home with Science

Dig and Sow!

How do plants grow?

Written by Janice Lobb

Illustrated by Peter Utton and Ann Savage

KINGFISHER

NEW YORK

KINGFISHER
a Houghton Mifflin Company imprint
215 Park Avenue South
New York, New York 10003
www.houghtonmifflinbooks.com

First published in hardcover in 2000
10 9 8 7 6 5 4 3 2
2TR/0701/FR/128MARWA

This edition first published in 2002
10 9 8 7 6 5 4 3 2 1
1TR/0502/SCPC/FR/128MA

Created and designed by Snapdragon Publishing Ltd.
Copyright © Snapdragon Publishing Ltd. 2000

LIBRARY OF CONGRESS CATALOGING-IN-PUBLICATION DATA
Lobb, Janice.
     Dig and sow! how do plants grow?/by Janice Lobb;
illustrated by Peter Utton.—1st ed.
         p.   cm. — (At home with science)
     Summary: Introduces various scientific principles about botany
and plants and presents simple experiments which illustrate them.
     ISBN 0-7534-5245-6 (HC)
     ISBN 0-7534-5459-9 (PB)
      1. Plants—Miscellanea—Juvenile literature. 2. Botany—
Miscellanea—Juvenile literature. 3. Plants—Experiments—Juvenile
literature. 4. Botany—Experiments—Juvenile literature. [1. Plants—
Experiments. 2. Botany—Experiments. 3. Experiments.] I. Utton,
Peter, ill. II. Title. III. At home with science (New York, N.Y.)

QK49 .L83 2000
580—DC21
                                       99-049919
Printed in Hong Kong

Author Janice Lobb
Illustrators Peter Utton and Ann Savage

For Snapdragon
Editorial Director Jackie Fortey
Art Director Chris Legee

For Kingfisher
Series Editors Camilla Reid and Emma Wild
Series Art Editor Mike Buckley

Contents

See for yourself!

1 Read about the science in your backyard, then try the "See for yourself!" experiments to discover how it works. In science, experiments try to find or show the answers.

2

Carefully read the instructions for each experiment, making sure you follow the numbered instructions in the correct order.

3 Here are some of the things you will need. Have everything ready before you start each experiment.

Fishing net

Plastic tray

Alfalfa seeds

Plastic bottle with cap

Glass jar

Small jars with lids

Magnifying glass

Plastic ruler

Red food coloring

4 Safety first! ✋

Some scientists took risks to make their discoveries, but our experiments are safe. Just make sure that you tell an adult what you are doing, and get their help when you see the red warning sign.

Amazing facts

WOW!

You'll notice that some words are written in *italics*. You can learn more about them in the glossary at the back of the book. And if you want to find out some amazing facts, keep an eye out for the "Wow!" panels.

Keep an eye out for useful tips!

Have fun!

Why is grass green?

Unlike animals, plants make their own food. They do this by absorbing the sun's *energy* and changing it into food. This process is called *photosynthesis*. In order to do this, plants need a substance called *chlorophyll*. Chlorophyll is green, which is why most plants are green.

The food factory

Plants use chlorophyll, *carbon dioxide*, and water to make a sugary food called *glucose*. As they do this, they release *oxygen* into the air.

Why are aliens good at gardening?

Because they have green thumbs!

Chlorophyll absorbs the sun's light

Carbon dioxide is taken from the air

Oxygen is released into the air

Water is taken in by the roots

Plants under rocks are pale and straggly. This is because they are growing in the dark and have not made any chlorophyll.

Archie can't make his own food and must eat plants to live. So, indirectly, his food comes from the sun, too.

Fresh air

Too much carbon dioxide in the air can suffocate animals, but plants love it. The oxygen in the air is produced by plants during photosynthesis. Without plants we would not be able to breathe at all. Trees in the world's forests, grass on the plains, and *algae* in the sea all help to keep the air fresh.

WOW!

See for yourself!

1 Watch photosynthesis happening for yourself. Collect some leaves, like laurel or geranium. New, fresh ones will work best.

2 Pour some water into a shallow bowl or plastic container and put the leaves in with their undersides facing up. To compare them, float one or two leaves the right way up.

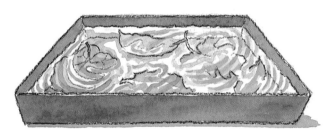

3 Leave them in the sunshine for a little while. Then look at them through a magnifying glass. You will see little bubbles of oxygen.

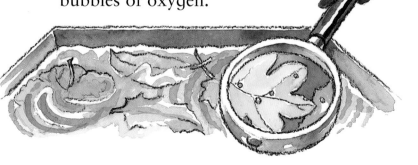

We all need to eat green plants to stay healthy.

Why don't trees fall down?

Why is an elephant like a tree?

Because they both have trunks!

Like most plants, trees need to grow upward to get as much light as possible. To keep them from falling down, plants have *roots* that spread out under the ground and support them as they grow. As well as supporting the plant, roots also suck up water from the soil. Trees need thick, woody roots to support their heavy trunks, but smaller plants have thinner roots.

A tree can grow tall because its stem is a firm trunk made of wood. Small flowering plants do not make wood. They need water in their stems to keep them from drooping.

Every year a new layer of wood grows on the outside of a tree's trunk, under the bark.

A tree

Woody trunk

Woody roots

You can tell how old a tree is by counting the growth rings in the trunk

A small flowering plant

Stem

Hairy roots

8

See for yourself!

1 Place a dandelion, a rose, a celery stalk, and some twigs into a jar of water. Then put identical plants in another jar without water.

2 Leave both jars for a couple of days, looking at them from time to time. What happens to the plants?

Without water

3 Even without water, woody stems stay stiff, but their flowers and leaves droop and shrivel.

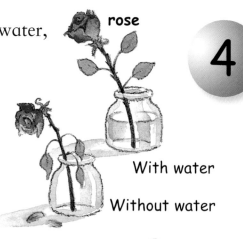

rose

With water

Without water

4 The stem of the dandelion is supported by the pressure of the water inside it. So, in a jar of water it stands up well, but left out of water it will droop and die within a few hours.

dandelion

With water

Without water

Big trunks

WOW!

In Africa, there is a tree called the baobab that has an unusual trunk. During the rainy season, the tree stores water inside the trunk, which swells up like a barrel. In dry weather, it uses this water to survive, and the trunk shrinks again.

Don't wait until you see your plants drooping before you water them.

9

What is soil?

Y ou know what soil is—it's the dark, crumbly stuff that you see under the grass in the backyard. But do you know what soil is made of? In fact, it is a mixture of a lot of things—small pieces of rock, *minerals*, air, and water, as well as the remains of dead plants and animals, which are called *humus*. All these different things are found in the layers that make up soil.

See for yourself!

1 Put a handful of soil in a jar. Fill it up with water and put the lid on tightly. Shake the jar and leave it to stand for a few minutes.

2 The soil should separate into several layers, with the heavier rocks at the bottom, and the lighter material, like leaves and twigs, at the top.

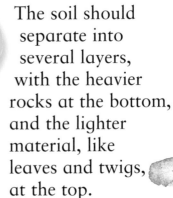

How is soil made?

Soil starts to form on the surface of bare rocks. Over time, the weather wears away the surface of the rock, flaking off small rock *particles*. These particles collect in cracks and crevices in the rock.

Small plants, such as *moss*, start to grow on top of the fragments of rock. When they die, they become part of the newly formed soil. This humus helps to hold the soil together.

Gradually, the soil gets thicker, and small animals can live in it. Earthworms help by mixing the rock particles and the humus. They also let in the air that the plant roots need to grow.

Rock particles collect in cracks in the rock

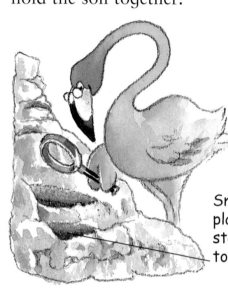

Small plants start to grow

Worms help to mix the new soil

WOW!

Sliding soil

Soil takes a long time to form, but it can be lost very quickly. When people cut down too many trees, the soil becomes loose and the wind can blow it away. It can also be washed away in a landslide if it rains a lot. This is called *erosion*.

Remember to wash the soil off your hands when you are finished.

Do plants eat and drink?

Although plants don't eat and drink like us, they do need food and water to survive. As we have discovered, they make their food from the sunshine and air. They drink by sucking up water from the soil through their long, wide-spreading roots. The roots also take in minerals such as magnesium that keep the plant healthy.

What do plants like to drink?

Root beer!

Keeping healthy

If there is not enough magnesium or iron in the soil, plants can't make enough green chlorophyll, and they turn yellow or white.

Gardeners use fertilizers such as manure to feed plants if the soil does not have enough minerals.

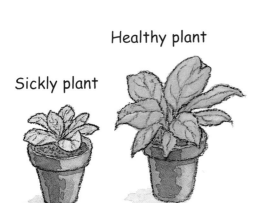

Sickly plant

Healthy plant

Manure

See for yourself!

1 Fill a glass with water and add a few drops of red food coloring. Cut the bottom off of a celery stalk and place it in the glass.

2 Leave it for about an hour and then take a look. You will see that the pink color has crept upward, carried by the water in the celery stalk.

3 Cut through the celery stalk and you will see the tubes that carry water and sap. Have they changed color?

4 You can try this with a white flower, like a carnation. If you leave it in the colored water long enough, the petals will turn pink too.

WOW! # Trapped!

The Venus flytrap grows in boggy soil that does not provide it with all the minerals it needs. The flytrap has developed an unusual way of adding to its diet—it waits for flies to land on its leaves, then snaps them shut and digests the fly.

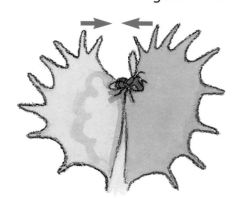

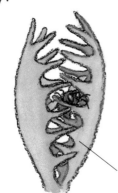

The leaves snap shut and trap the fly

Cut flowers need to be put in water to stay fresh.

13

What are flowers for?

Flowers look pretty in the backyard, but they also perform a useful job. They contain the parts of the plant that make *seeds*. These seeds will grow into new plants. Most flowering plants need help making their seeds. Some use insects to carry their *pollen* from one flower to another. The bright colors and scents of flowers encourage bees and other insects to visit them. Other plants, like grasses, use the wind to carry pollen.

Why is a flower like the letter A?

Because a B comes after it!

How a seed is made

As it searches for *nectar*, the bee rubs against the *stamens*, the male parts of the flower, and picks up fine yellow grains of pollen.

When it flies to the next flower, the bee rubs against the *carpels*, the female parts of the plant, leaving the pollen behind.

The grains of pollen stick to the carpels and then move down to join the tiny egg cells inside. These will soon become seeds.

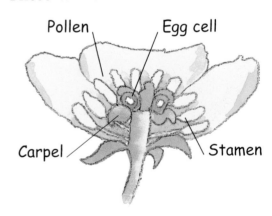

Pollen

Egg cell

Carpel

Stamen

14

See for yourself! ✋

1 Look at a flower bud. Around the outside are green *sepals*, which protect the flower when it is growing.

Sepal

Sepal

2 Now look at a flower. The bright *petals*, which can be white or colored, attract insects to the flower.

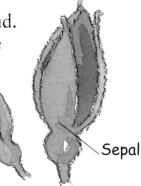

Petal

3 Inside the flower are the stamens, which stick up from the center. Try shaking them onto dark paper to see if they leave a yellow dust.

Stamen

4 Find a flower that is losing its petals and cut it in half. (Ask an adult to help you do this.) Can you see all the different parts the plant uses to make seeds?

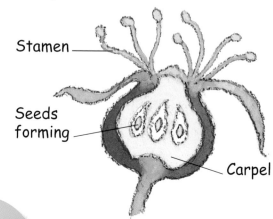

Stamen

Seeds forming

Carpel

Fruity packages

WOW!

The fruit is the part of a plant that carries and protects the seeds. Fruits can be juicy, like tomatoes and bell peppers, or dry, like poppy capsules. You can see the seeds in a tomato or a bell pepper that has been cut in half.

Seed

To keep a rosebush blooming, cut off the dead flower heads.

15

Where do plants come from?

Every country has plants that grow there naturally. We call these *native* plants. You may find some of them in the countryside or in a wildflower area. Some plants grow where we don't want them. We call these plants *weeds*. When explorers went to new countries, they brought plants back with them. When people settled in new places, they often took plants with them. Plants that come from different places are called *introduced plants*. So you might have plants from many countries in your backyard.

What did one plant say to the other plant?

Have we been introduced?

How plants spread

When a plant is growing well in one place, it flowers and makes seeds. These help the plant spread to new places.

Other seeds are eaten by animals and birds, and pass through their bodies.

Some seeds are carried away from the parent plant by the wind or rain.

See for yourself!

1 Pick a dandelion and blow on it. See how far the seeds go before they reach the ground. The little fluffy parachute at the top of each seed helps it float in the air.

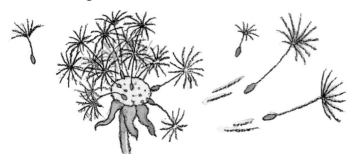

2 Look out for tiny seeds and other seeds with parachutes or wings. Are they shot through the air, or do they "fly" or spin?

Seeds with wings

3 Look for seeds that hook on to animal fur or your clothes. Can you find larger seeds that roll away from the plants?

4 Look out for seeds in mud on your shoes or on the wheels of your bicycle.

WOW!

Seeds ahoy!

Coconut palms grow along sandy beaches on tropical islands. The coconuts are their seeds. If a coconut falls into the sea, it can float many miles to another island, where it might *germinate* and grow.

Never touch berries you don't know—they may be poisonous!

17

How do seeds grow?

Every seed has the beginnings of a new plant inside it, waiting to grow. This is called an *embryo*. In the spring, when there is plenty of sun and rain, the seed starts to grow. Using the special supply of food stored inside the seed, a little *shoot* grows toward the sunlight, while a root grows down, looking for water. When a seed starts to grow, we say it germinates.

What did the frost say to the seed?

Don't shoot!

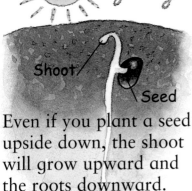

Shoot

Seed

Even if you plant a seed upside down, the shoot will grow upward and the roots downward.

Roots

The shoot grows quickly, feeding off the food stored inside its seed.

Plants grow toward the sun

When the shoot reaches the light, it starts to make its own food with help from the sun.

See for yourself!

1 Line a tray with a paper towel. Wet it with warm water and sprinkle some alfalfa seeds on it.

2 Find a box big enough to hold the tray. Cut a window in the lower half of one end. Put the tray inside and close the lid.

3 Put the box in a warm, light place and keep the seeds moist with water.

4 Do the alfalfa sprouts grow straight up or do they grow toward the sunlight that comes in from the side of the box?

WOW!

Running plants

Some plants produce baby plants instead of seeds. Strawberry plants and spider plants put out *runners*. These are long stems that grow along the ground. At the end of each stem is a miniature plant complete with leaves and roots. This will grow if you plant it in a pot of soil.

Try growing a plant from an apple or avocado seed.

19

Do plants die in the winter?

What has eyes but cannot see?

A potato!

Winter is a hard time for plants. There is not enough sunshine to give them energy. They can't get enough water from frozen soil. Winds batter them and they may break under the weight of snow. *Deciduous* plants store food in the summer, then shed their leaves in the fall. Small plants may die back to ground level. The parts of the plant that are left bare or underground rest through the winter. Plants that die after they flower leave seeds that grow into new plants.

Storing food

The food stored in seeds is used when they start to grow, or germinate.

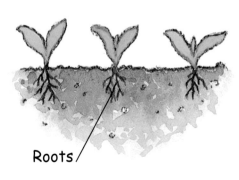

Roots

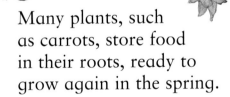

Bulb

Swollen bases of leaves and stems, called bulbs, store food under the ground. Bulbs help plants grow again in the spring.

Many plants, such as carrots, store food in their roots, ready to grow again in the spring.

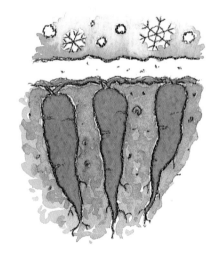

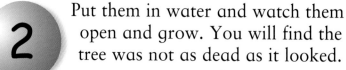

See for yourself!

1 Pick twigs in winter or early spring. You can see the buds that will grow into new leaves and flowers. Some, like horse chestnuts, have sticky buds.

2 Put them in water and watch them open and grow. You will find the tree was not as dead as it looked.

3 Look in the vegetable drawer. Each "eye" on a potato, each clove of garlic, is a bud waiting to grow into a new plant.

4 Try leaving vegetables in a dark cabinet for a couple of weeks. They will start to sprout and shoots will begin to grow.

Garlic clove

Eye

Desert flowers

WOW!

There are plants that make seeds so that they can live through very hot, dry weather. These seeds can lie for years in desert soil. Then, when rain comes, they germinate and flower, bringing color to the desert landscape.

Soak a bean and open it to see the baby plant inside.

What do worms do all day?

Earthworms may not look like busy creatures, but in fact they work very hard. Worms feed by swallowing soil as they burrow. At night, they pull dead plants from the surface down under the ground with their mouths. All this activity is good for the soil and for the plants living in it. It helps to get rid of dead plants and to bring air to the roots of the living ones.

How can you tell where a worm's head is?

Tickle its tummy and see which end laughs!

Wood louse

Worm cast

Leaf being pulled down

Worm burrow

Mouth

An earthworm wriggles along by changing the shape of its body segments

Bristles

Segment

The worm stretches out parts of its body

and then pulls the rest along

See for yourself!

1 To make a wormery, find a large jar (like a pickle jar). Place a plastic bottle inside it with the cap on it. (You can leave out the bottle if your jar is small.)

2 Fill the jar (but not the bottle) with layers of sand, soil, and compost, then finish off with some dead leaves. Cover the sides of the jar with dark paper.

3 Find three or four earthworms and put them in the top. Stretch a layer of netting across the mouth of the jar and fasten with a rubber band.

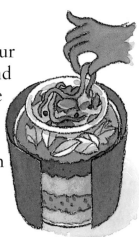

4 Put the jar in a cool place and make sure that the soil stays damp, but not soggy. After a few days, check to see what has happened to the soil.

Worm burrows

You should find that the worms have mixed the layers of sand and soil

Giant worms!

WOW!

One of the world's largest earthworms lives near creeks in the Bass River Valley, in the southern Australian state of Victoria. The Giant Gippsland earthworm can grow to over 4 yards long and makes a gurgling sound as it slides through its tunnels. Giant earthworms are rare, so there are laws to protect them.

Set your worms free when you are finished with them.

23

Why do bees hum?

Why does a bee hum?

Because it has forgotten the words!

Bees and many other insects hum or buzz. They make the noise with their wings when they fly. Although insect wings look delicate, they are quite stiff. When the wings flap down, the air under them is pushed out of the way in little puffs. This lifts the insect up into the air. When the wings flap up, the air above them is moved away. The way the wings move makes the air *vibrate*. When these little puffs of air reach our ears, we hear them as sound.

See for yourself!

1 You can make the air vibrate. Take a piece of thin plastic, such as a ruler, and wave it back and forth quickly near your face. Can you feel the air moving in little puffs?

2 Then put the ruler on the table so that about three fourths of it sticks out beyond the table edge. Hold down one end firmly with one hand. Bend the other end and let go of it quickly. Can you hear a sound?

Sizes and sounds

Mosquitoes have little wings that make the air vibrate very fast. This action makes a very high, whining sound.

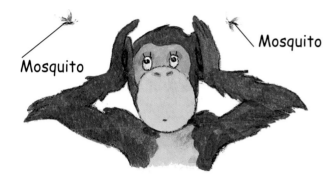

Mosquito

Mosquito

The bumblebee's larger wings make the air vibrate more slowly. This makes a low buzzing sound.

Bee

3 Now place the ruler on the table so that only half of it sticks out and repeat. Then a fourth. Listen to the different sounds made by the ruler moving through the air. Like a bee's wings, the ruler makes the air vibrate.

You can't hear the sound made by a butterfly's wings, because they flap too slowly.

Butterfly

WOW!

Musical legs

Not all insects make sounds with their wings. Grasshoppers and crickets chirp. To do this, they make the air vibrate by rubbing their back legs against the edges of their hard *wing cases*.

Remember that bees and wasps can sting—so look but don't touch!

Who visits the backyard?

Most animals spend their daily lives in a constant search for food. If there is not enough food where they live, the animals must travel to find it, and your backyard may be one of the places that they visit. Sit quietly in a corner of the yard and watch the visitors as they come and go. They may fly in, they may come up from the ground, or they may get in under a fence or hedge. Some will be more welcome than others!

> Why wasn't the butterfly invited to the dance?

> Because it was a moth ball!

Keep an eye out

Butterflies and bees are attracted to the scent and color of flowers. They drink the flowers' nectar.

Aphid

Ladybug

Ladybugs are good insects to have around. They eat the aphids that feed on— and ruin—many plants.

Woodpeckers look for ants and other insects on the lawn. Other birds, like pigeons, look for seeds and snails.

Pigeon

Woodpecker

See for yourself!

1 In the winter, when food is scarce, you can help your local wildlife by putting food out for them. A range of food will attract a variety of creatures. Avoid giving birds bread, which is bad for them.

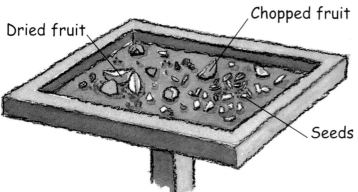

Dried fruit

Chopped fruit

Seeds

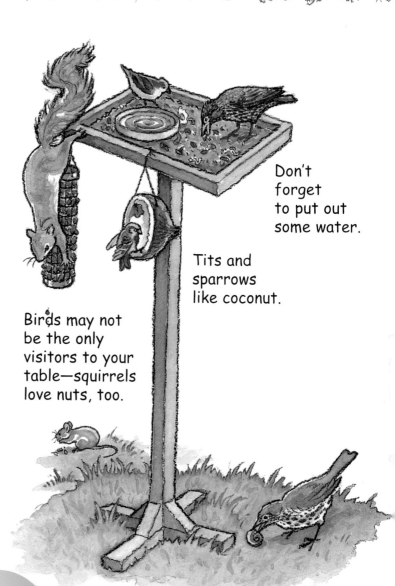

Don't forget to put out some water.

Tits and sparrows like coconut.

Birds may not be the only visitors to your table—squirrels love nuts, too.

2 Make a note of what animals you see and how often they visit your backyard.

WOW!

Nighttime visitors

Many animals come and go while you are asleep. If you live in the country or near the woods, your backyard might be visited by foxes, raccoons, deer, or rabbits. Keep an eye out for the tracks and droppings they leave behind.

Make a conservation corner in your backyard for wildlife to visit.

27

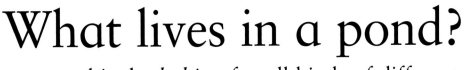

What lives in a pond?

A pond is the *habitat* for all kinds of different plants and animals. This means that the pond gives them food, water, and shelter—all the things they need to survive. Some plants live at the bottom of the pond. Others float on the surface or live on the banks. The plants make oxygen which keeps the water fresh for the animals that live there. Small animals such as pond snails feed on the plants, and frogs lay their *frogspawn* in them. The frogspawn hatches into tadpoles, which turn into frogs.

Where do fish sleep?

In water beds!

Baby tadpoles nibble weeds

Frogspawn

Toadspawn

Older tadpoles feed on tiny animals

See for yourself! ✋

1 With an adult's help, get some pond water. Then fish out some pondweed using a net. Be very careful not to fall in!

2 Put some of the pond water in a deep, white bowl. Using a magnifying glass, look closely at what is floating and swimming around in the water.

Mosquito larva

Algae

Water flea

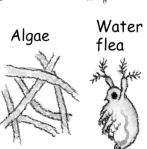

3 Now add the pondweed to your bowl. Can you see any tiny creatures hiding in it?

Pond snail

Weed

4 Sit quietly by the pond to see what other insects you can spot. Where are they? How do they move around?

Dragonfly

Whirligig beetle

Water boatman

Walking on water!

WOW!

Some insects, such as water striders, are able to glide quickly over the surface of still water. A force called *surface tension* keeps them from sinking into the water. It makes the water behave as if it were covered by a thin, elastic skin.

Be sure to return the pond creatures to their home.

29

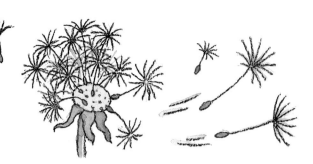

Backyard quiz

1 What do you call the substance that makes leaves green?
a) Iron
b) Chlorophyll
c) Carbon dioxide

2 How can you find out how old a tree is?
a) By counting its roots
b) By counting its branches
c) By counting the rings in its trunk

3 Where can you find a layer of humus?
a) In the soil
b) In the air
c) In leaves

4 What does a Venus flytrap eat?
a) Nectar
b) Insects
c) Frogs

5 What do bees carry from one flower to another?
a) Carpels
b) Pollen
c) Seeds

6 How does a dandelion spread its seeds?
a) It uses the sun
b) It uses the sea
c) It uses the wind

7 What does a seed do when it germinates?
a) It dies
b) It begins to grow
c) It spreads its seeds

8 How does a bulb help a plant live through the winter?
a) By spreading seeds
b) By losing leaves
c) By storing food

9 What does an earthworm use to pull leaves down into the soil?
a) Its mouth
b) Its tail
c) Its segments

10 Which of these insects walks on water?
a) The water strider
b) The bee
c) The butterfly

30

Answers on page 32

Glossary

Algae
Plants that grow in water or on moist ground, and have no stems, leaves, or flowers.

Carbon dioxide
A gas found in the air, which is used by green plants in photosynthesis.

Carpels
The female parts of a flower, which contain the egg cell.

Chlorophyll
The green pigment in plants that absorbs energy from the sun.

Deciduous
Deciduous trees and shrubs lose their leaves in the fall.

Embryo
A baby plant that starts to grow inside a seed.

Energy
The ability to do work or make something happen.

Erosion
The wearing away of rock and soil by the weather.

Frogspawn
A mass of frog's eggs protected by jelly and laid in water.

Germinate
To begin to grow, by sprouting a new plant from a seed.

Glucose
The sugary food that green plants make during photosynthesis.

Habitat
The natural home of a plant or animal.

Humus
A substance made from decayed plants, leaves, and animal matter.

Introduced plants
Plants that are brought from one area to another by humans.

Minerals
Chemicals that are found naturally in rocks and soil, which do not come from living things.

Moss
Small flowerless plants that grow as a thick mass on rocks or tree trunks.

Native
Plants or animals that grow naturally in a particular place or area.

Nectar
A sugary fluid found at the base of flower petals, which attracts insects and birds.

Oxygen
A gas in the air that animals need to breathe, made by green plants during photosynthesis.

Particle
A very small piece of something.

Petals
The outer parts of a flower, used mainly to attract feeding insects.

Photosynthesis
The way in which green plants make food, using energy from the sun.

Pollen
Tiny grains made by flowers, which contain male sex cells. When they join with female egg cells, they produce seeds.

Root
The part of a plant or tree found underground.

Runners
Stems that grow flat on the ground, and produce baby plants at the tips.

Seed
The part of a plant from which a new plant grows.

Sepals
The outer, green parts of a flower bud that protect petals as they develop.

Shoot
A new plant that grows from a seed; or a young stem with leaves and buds.

Stamens
The male parts of a plant, which produce pollen.

Surface tension
A force that makes the surface of water behave like an elastic skin.

Vibrate
To move back and forth very quickly.

Weed
A plant that grows wild or unwanted among cultivated plants.

Wing cases
In insects, hard front wings that are used to protect the hind wings, not for flying.

Index

Answers to the Backyard quiz on page 30
1 b **2** c **3** a **4** b **5** b **6** c **7** b **8** c **9** a **10** a